Faith, Reason, and the New Mass Translation.

Faith, Reason, and the New Mass Translation.

by John C. Wilhelmsson

Wilhelmsson

Chaos To Order Publishing

San Jose, California

Faith, Reason, and the New Mass Translation.

Copyright © 2014
John C. Wilhelmsson
All rights reserved.
ISBN: 0988656388
ISBN-13: 978-0988656383

Wilhelmsson

DEDICATION

For Saint John Paul II
The Pope of Faith and Reason.
Upon his Canonization
April 27, 2014.

Wilhelmsson

FOREWORD

What follows are my reflections on the 2011 translation change, which was in reality the loss, of the English version of the Novus Ordo Mass. The reflections are my own yet I think are, in principle, shared by many. For the 1969 Novus Ordo Mass was the primary way of worship for Catholics in the English speaking world for 42 years. And I, for one, will not allow the thing that shaped us to just be quietly swept away.

Faith, Reason, and the New Mass Translation.

WWW.C2OP.COM

Faith, Reason, and the New Mass Translation.

Faith, Reason, and the New Mass Translation.

CONTENTS

Introduction
1

The Backstory
7

And Also With You
23

Faith And Reason
31

The Old "We Believe" Crowd
39

A $5 Word Can Be Costly
47

The All And The Many
55

A Tale Of Two Traditions
67

Teaching Authority
79

Conclusion
85

Wilhelmsson

Faith, Reason, and the New Mass Translation.

INTRODUCTION

In Advent of 2011 the Catholic Church changed the Mass from the clear modern English of the Novus Ordo Mass to an obtuse literal translation from the Latin. By a long established theological principle known as "Lex Orandi, Lex Credendi" this change in the prayer of the Church also brought with it a change in the belief of the Church.

I began writing this book after a conversation with a fellow Catholic about the new Mass translation. She told me that the new changes were "only words." Yet as a person who has studied both theology and philosophy and spoken on them many times before many different types of Catholic groups I sadly realized that this is simply not the case.

Faith, Reason, and the New Mass Translation.

For there is a principle in theology known as "Lex Orandi, Lex Credendi" which in English means, "as we pray so we believe." This principle is often invoked in theology to show historic evidence for a doctrine. For if one can show evidence in history that a special Mass was dedicated to a particular doctrine early on then the early prayer of said Mass can then be used as a direct evidence for the early belief of said doctrine.

Thus the new English translation of the Mass does matter. For by a long held theological principle a new prayer does in fact bring with it a new belief. How will the new translation of the Mass change Catholic belief? What forces were behind the change? What is the history of this whole issue? These are just a few of the questions we shall reflect upon in this book.

Faith, Reason, and the New Mass Translation.

In the time since the change was made I have come to realize that the Novus Ordo Mass of 1973 was in reality not just the center of my faith but also my emotional centre in an ever changing world. The one place that I could always go back to and that always spoke to and nourished me. Thus it is not at all surprising that my reaction to its loss has been spirited.

I began writing in this spirited way in a series of "Faith and Reason" blogs. I thought about all the things I missed about the Novus Ordo Mass of 1973 and the, perhaps, sometimes hidden yet profound meaning within it. I went through the issues one by one and soon found that I had a good deal of material down. And in the midst of all of this writing I began to feel a sense of healing.

Faith, Reason, and the New Mass Translation.

Thus I offer this little book both as a serious discussion about the state of the Church today and as a sort of emotional therapy for all those who, like me, are now being forced to live without something that was in at the center of their lives. And even more than this, at the center of the particularly beautiful culture of reason and communal spirit that sprang forth form the Novus Ordo Mass of 1973.

I offer it as well to all the Catholic bishops in the English speaking world. So that those who are our spiritual shepherds might once again hear the cries of their sheep. For we are not sheep who ran away but who were lost. And we would gladly wish to return to the fold if only we might once again hear the familiar calls of our youth.

Faith, Reason, and the New Mass Translation.

Faith, Reason, and the New Mass Translation.

Faith, Reason, and the New Mass Translation.

THE BACKSTORY

On May 5th 1988 Cardinal Joseph Ratzinger signed an accord with Archbishop Marcel Lefebvre designed to bring the latter's group of extreme traditionalists into communion with the Catholic Church. For reasons perhaps now lost to history, Lefebvre tore up the accord the next day thus ending all hope of an agreement. Two months later in his Apostolic Letter *Ecclesia Dei* Pope John Paul II informed the Archbishop that he and his associates had brought upon themselves the grave penalty of excommunication for illegitimately ordaining their own bishops that past June 30th.[i]

This little known event of ecclesiastic history might seem

Faith, Reason, and the New Mass Translation.

insignificant in itself without understanding the issues that brought it about and the players who were involved. Cardinal Ratzinger would, of course, go on to become Pope Benedict XVI in 2005. And it is said that perhaps the greatest regret he brought with him into that office was the failed accord with Lefebvre and the subsequent excommunication of him and his extreme traditionalists followers.

Yet just who were the Lefebvrites and why do I call them extreme traditionalists? I reserve the term for those who reject the Second Vatican Council as an authentic council of the Church and thus wish to go back to a pre-conciliar time. To such people the Second Vatican Council's stated goal to open the Church up to the modern world, and in particular its decision to do this through a reform of the liturgy, were quite simply unacceptable. For they see the Council not as much as a spiritual event but as a political event in which the liberals triumphed over the conservatives. And their particular disdain in this regard is reserved for the liturgical reforms of Vatican II.[ii]

Thus the Novus Ordo Mass of 1973 with its clear modern English translation became a particular target of theirs. In fact, the Novus Ordo Mass of 1973 came under such immediate attack that on January 25th 1974 the Congregation for the Doctrine of the Faith was forced to clarify that there was no doubt whatsoever regarding the validity of Masses celebrated using "for all" as a translation of "pro multis" during the words of consecration rather than "for many".[iii]

[The great irony of this for us today being that the new Mass translation reverses this very change that the Congregation for the Doctrine of the Faith clarified as proper in 1974].

Traditionalists like the Lefebvrites grew strong in the wake of the Council through appealing to the many liturgically traditional Catholics who had been displaced by the reforms of Vatican II. And their formidable strength quite early on can be seen in the fact that a clarification of the validity of the 1973 Novus Ordo Mass was needed so quickly.

It seems to me that there is an important lesson for the Church to learn from history here. For the great majority of the people who flocked to the traditionalists movements did not do so because the Novus Ordo Mass existed as such, but rather because it existed as the only exclusive option available. Thus if early on they would have been given a choice of still worshiping in the way they had become accustomed to movements like the Lefebvrites most likely never would have gained traction.

However, at the time no such option was given and the faithful were faced with the choice of either abandoning their way of worship or leaving the Church altogether. Thus, groups like the Lefebvrites stepped into this vacuum and began to grow so quickly that they soon became a problem. By the time Pope Benedict XVI issued his instruction allowing for the greater use of the traditional Latin Mass in July 2007 it was a classic case of too little and far too late.[iv]

In any case, the Church rather than learning from the past seems to have become haunted by it. Particularly with regard to Cardinal Ratzinger who many believe saw the Lefebvrite schism as a personal failing. A failing so great that he was later willing to use his office as Pope Benedict XVI to attempt to fix it.

One can offer as evidence of this a quite curious act he engaged in as Pope Benedict XVI in 2009. For on January 24th of that year, to the great shock of many, he lifted the excommunications of the four Lefebvrite bishops that had been put in place by Pope John Paul II in 1988. This even in the face of charges made by several mainline Jewish groups that one of the Lefebvrite bishops was in fact a holocaust denier.[v]

Faith, Reason, and the New Mass Translation.

In fact, some interpret the 2007 instruction allowing for the greater use of the traditional Latin Mass, the 2009 lifting of the excommunications of the Lefebvrite bishops, and the 2011 new English Mass translation as the three major events in a pattern of behavior designed to appease the extreme traditionalists movements.

The history of the new English Mass translation itself seems to offer evidence that even a more long-term pattern of appeasement may have been in place. The International Commission on English in the Liturgy (ICEL) was set up in 1963 in anticipation of an English vernacular Mass being needed. And, although Pope Paul VI first promulgated the Novus Ordo Mass in 1969, a translation of it most fully into the

English vernacular did not appear until 1973. Later, in 1983, the ICEL began work on a second English translation of the Mass in hopes of producing a more poetic yet still literary translation. After a great deal of work and negotiation this version was finally approved by all of the English speaking conferences of Catholic bishops in 1998 and then sent off to the Vatican for approval.

However, in 2001 the Vatican Congregation for Divine Worship issued a new instruction on translation, *Liturgiam Authenticam*, which called for a literal, rather than a literary, translation of the Latin.[vi] The ICEL was then purged of those in favor of a modern literary translation and they were replaced by new, handpicked by the Vatican, members in favor of a literal translation from the Latin text.

Faith, Reason, and the New Mass Translation.

Therefore, if you are wondering why the new English translation of the Mass seems so foreign to us here in the English speaking Catholic world one need look no further than at the aforementioned facts. For the new English translation of the Mass is, in fact, not a legitimate expression of the English speaking Catholic world but rather that of a Vatican Congregation!

The reform of the translation approved by all of the English speaking conferences of bishops and sent to Rome in 1998 was hardly perfect. For in the years since 1973 some questionable changes had been made by the ICEL. However, the fact that the work of a legitimate local authority was summarily trashed by a Vatican Congregation is most troubling with regard to the principle of Subsidiarity. The Catechism of the Catholic Church (CCC) describes Subsidiarity in the following way:

> *The teaching of the Church has elaborated the principle of subsidiarity, according to which "a community of a higher order should not interfere in the internal life of a community of a lower order, depriving the latter of its functions, but rather should support it in case of need and help to co- ordinate its activity with the activities of the rest of society, always with a view to the common good."1 perhaps the most important principle of Catholic Social Justice. It states that, in so far as it is possible, issues should be resolved on the local level.[vii]*

In this case the English speaking bishops put forth a process on the local level and carefully carried it out over time. They then arrived at a consensus about the translation and sent it off to the Vatican Congregation for Divine Worship for approval. The Vatican Congregation for Divine Worship sat on the issue for a time, refusing to issue an approval or a rejection, and then basically changed the rules of the game. That their actions were a violation of the principle of Subsidiarity is not in doubt. That their actions were further a violation of the right of the English speaking Catholic bishops to care for the souls of their flocks seems quite apparent to me as well.

The fact that this interference in bringing about a second English translation happened in the context of the Vatican wishing to appease extreme traditionalists groups, like the Lefebvrites, makes it reek more of a back room political machination than an authentic movement of the Spirit. And for this reason, Catholics in the English speaking world are now suffering not only under an archaic translation of the Mass which is not the expression of themselves or their bishops, but also under the knowledge that the process that brought this all about was hardly a spiritual one. And the scandal that this faulty process has caused among the faithful is at least as serious of an issue as the archaic new English Mass translation itself.

The irony now is that the Lefebvrites seem to have had everything they wanted handed to them on a silver platter. For it was the extreme traditionalists who challenge "for all" back in 1974 and wanted it changed to "for many" (as the new Mass translation has now done). And it is the extreme traditionalist who would obviously favor a literal translation from the Latin (as the new Mass translation has now also done). Yet, even after all of this, the Lefebvrites still refuse accord. This is the greatest evidence of all that this whole sordid affair was indeed not an authentic movement of the Spirit but, rather, a political calculation designed to appease extreme traditionalists. For the fruit of the Spirit is unity, while the fruit of back room machinations can only be further division.

Faith, Reason, and the New Mass Translation.

Faith, Reason, and the New Mass Translation.

THE FAITH AND REASON BLOGS

Faith, Reason, and the New Mass Translation.

AND ALSO WITH YOU

The first difference one notices in the new Mass translation is something which starts at the beginning and then occurs several times throughout the Mass. The greeting of the priest to the people "peace be with you" remains the same yet the response has changed from "and also with you" to "and with your spirit." While on the face of it this seems like a small change to a more literal translation from the Latin there are actually several things going on here.

The stated purpose of the Second Vatican Council was to "open up the windows" of the church to the modern world. Yet what do I mean by "modern"? That is a rather complex question in itself.

In the discipline of philosophy we

speak of Descartes as being the first "modern" philosopher. If one had to give a quick description of what Descartes did, as a philosophy professor must sometimes do, it would be that he turned the discussion about philosophy into what was going on in the subjective experience of the human person, and that he wrote his works not in the Latin of the universities but in the everyday French of his time.

We see here two themes emerging. First, relating things to people where they are at in their everyday subjective experience. And, second, speaking to people clearly in their everyday vernacular language. Therefore, if I had to give a quick definition of "modern" this would be it.

[It is important to note here that

Faith, Reason, and the New Mass Translation.

Descartes was not opposed by the Church in his method but actually supported by both his good friend Father Marin Mersenne and the great mystic and spiritual writer Cardinal Pierre de Bérulle].

The old form of "and also with you" was an everyday response which implied an equality between the two parties involved (the priest and the lay person). In a certain sense it set the tone for a Church community that was not top-down dominated by clerics but instead was more of a community of faith with both clerics and lay people moving forward side by side. The new form "and with your spirit" is no doubt closer in literal translation to the Latin "et cum spiritu tuo." Yet the purpose of a modern translation and a literal translation are two very different things. And in a certain sense this is the crux of the entire matter.

Was the Second Vatican Council about opening up the Church to the modern world or was it about translating the Latin of the Mass literally into the vernacular? I think anybody who has read the documents of Vatican II and wishes to be intellectually honest about them would say that the answer is the former. After all one of the central documents of the Second Vatican Council is in fact entitled "The Church in the Modern World."

Another more complex issue within this seemingly simple change involves Church politics. For anyone who has worked in, or even been around, the Church knows about the at times ugly nature of Church politics. And, indeed, one of the most ugly

Faith, Reason, and the New Mass Translation.

parts of recent Church politics has had to do with something called "clericalism." "Clericalism" basically means that, at times in the past and perhaps even still now, lay people have put clerics so far up on a pedestal and so far beyond questioning and accountability that bad things have happened.

I do not wish to open up fresh wounds here but it seems to me that recently some clerics felt that they were so high up on a pedestal that some shameful abuses, some even involving children, occurred. And it, further, seems to me that the Church is still in the process of trying to recover from these scandals. For these reasons it seems like a very inappropriate time to change the translation of the basic liturgical call and response between clerics and lay people to a formula which, at least, puts clerics on an unequal basis with lay people and, at worst, puts clerics up on a pedestal once again!

If the Church has not learned this very basic common sense lesson from the recent scandals how can we ever hope to prevent such things from happening again? In fact, now more than ever, clerics and lay people need to move forward together in a community of equality and accountability. And the beautiful call and response between the priest and lay people of the Novus Ordo Mass of 1973 is far more in keeping with such equality and accountability than the new Mass translation which has now been forced upon us!

Faith, Reason, and the New Mass Translation.

Faith, Reason, and the New Mass Translation.

FAITH AND REASON

As a philosophy professor I have the privilege of spending time reflecting in a special way on the meaning of everyday sort of words. Mainly because I have to teach certain concepts to my students (who actually often help me in clarifying their meaning). One of these words is "reason." Why do I call it an "everyday" sort of word? Because you very often hear people say things like "be reasonable" or "where is the reason in that?" Yet just what does "reason" mean?

There is funny thing about reason which many people fail to consider. It is that for a given act to be in accord with reason there is something you must absolutely know about the person engaging in said act. I often give my students this example: If they were to come into the classroom one morning and they saw me eating ice cream while they might think it curious they would most likely not think of it as being an unreasonable act. However, if I had a publically stated goal to lose 5 pounds by the end of the month and then they saw me eating ice cream they would be quite correct in saying: "Professor Wilhelmsson, that seems like an unreasonable act to me."

What is the difference between the two cases? Quite simply, in the first case they do not understand the goal or end of my actions while in the second case they do. Therefore, we see here that the reasonableness of an act and its goal or end are quite directly connected. As a matter of fact one can almost always say that one cannot understand whether an act is

Faith, Reason, and the New Mass Translation.

reasonable or not without understanding the actor's goal or end.

One of the most beautiful things about the old 1973 Novus Ordo Mass to me was that I was able to engage in it without offending my sense of reason (something one unfortunately can not say about the new Mass). Yet what do I mean by this? In the old Novus Ordo Mass of 1973 if the goal or end of a given act was to respond to the call "Peace be with you" I was able to respond in a quite reasonable way in modern English and say, "And also with you." Further, when I was about to engage in the act of receiving the real presence of the Lord at Communion I was able to say in a modern English anyone could understand, "Lord, I am not worthy to receive you, but only say the word and I shall be healed." Yet now I am asked to say, "Lord, I am not worthy that you should enter under my roof, but only say the word and my soul shall be healed." Not to go into the insensitivity toward homeless persons (who, in fact, do not have a roof to enter under), but the whole "roof" thing is simply not something a reasonable modern person might say given the goal or end of the act.

And even more troubling than this is that the whole "roof" thing takes one of the most touching and beautiful moments of the Mass away. So in that moment when I use to be in awe of the closeness and mercy of the Lord, I am now disturbed that I might be offending the poorest of the poor and am left wondering, "Where is this roof I am talking about anyhow?"

Why is this so important? It is

Faith, Reason, and the New Mass Translation.

important because we as Catholics are called to use both faith and reason. It is important to me as a philosopher because I really chose to go into the field of philosophy based upon the encyclical *Fide et Ratio* by Pope John Paul II.

In this encyclical he writes: "Faith and reason are like two wings on which the human spirit rises to the contemplation of truth." He then goes on to say that what is lacking in the Church today is not as much faith as it is reason! A remarkable statement for a Pope to have made (and which now, unfortunately, seems to have become a prophetic one).

In the advent of the implementation of the new Mass translation and all of the interesting stories I have been told by those seeking to "educate" me on them one would think that our late Holy Father had written a letter in 1998 entitled "Faith and Rationalization" rather than "Faith and Reason."

When I put things in perspective I realize that for my entire adult life, up until Advent of 2011, I was able to worship in the beautiful way of the Novus Ordo Mass of 1973. A Mass in which the sacred words were at the same time words of reason. Why the Church has changed this just at a time when it's stated goal is a new evangelization I have no idea.
All I can do now is respectfully say: "Professor, that seems like an unreasonable act to me."

Faith, Reason, and the New Mass Translation.

Faith, Reason, and the New Mass Translation.

Faith, Reason, and the New Mass Translation.

THE OLD "WE BELIEVE" CROWD

The new Mass translation changes the "We believe" in the Creed to an "I believe." Here is the old opening paragraph:

> "We believe in one God, the Father, the Almighty, maker of heaven and earth, of all that is seen and unseen."

And here is the new opening paragraph;

> "I believe in one God, the Father the Almighty, maker of heaven and earth, of all things visible and invisible."

It is interesting to speculate what the

logic behind this change might be?

On the face of things it seems rather odd to ask a congregation of people to come together (in reality oblige them to come together) and say a creed in unison which begins with the words "I believe." Should not, given the setting, the congregation say together as a whole "We believe" as was done in the old Novus Ordo mass of 1973? Now if the Creed is being recited in private it makes perfect sense for a person to say "I believe." But in public? (To further bear out how strange, and inaccurate, this change is the Greek of the Nicene Creed of the 4th century has *"pistoveumon,"* we believe, and not *"pisteuvo,"* I believe, as the first word of the Creed).

The old Novus Ordo Mass of 1973

had many features which suggested the idea of a community of faith equal in nature moving forward together. The call and response of the priest and lay people, "Peace be with you", "and also with you" The "We believe" of the old Creed rather than the "I believe" of the new. And there is even a third area where the focus has been put more on the individual than the community.

The addition to the Penitential Rite, which in other terms has changed very little, of the "through my fault, through my fault, through my most grievous fault" gives a definite added emphasis to individual sin (and thus to the individual). Thankfully, the most beautiful and reasonable phrase of: "in my thoughts and in my words, in what I have done, and in what I have failed to do," along with the wonderful communal aspect of the prayer: 'I ask blessed Mary ever-virgin, all the angels and saints, and you, my brothers and sisters, to pray for me to the lord our God" has not been changed significantly. Yet one still must wonder at the reasoning behind obliging a group of people to come together and then having them pray as if they were alone?

I have no doubt that some well-trained cleric or apologist for the new Mass translation could explain to me why my common sense is wrong here. Perhaps they could also share with me their copy of "Faith and Rationalization" (because apparently I really need to read that thing). My appraisals here are admittedly not those of a theologian. Theologians are wonderful yet there are just not all that many of them around. So I think it is better to appraise things from the perspective of common sense.

Philosophically speaking we think of this idea of common sense as that of being attentive to the phenomenal aspect of the experience. This is a rather technical area in itself yet what it basically means is that one should attempt to block out any "blinders" or prejudices about a given phenomenon and then just observe that phenomenon for what it is.

Why do we need to do this? I would say that if the Church wishes to attain the end or goal of a new evangelization it would be reasonable for it to start considering how the phenomenon of its main liturgy appears to a modern person. For there may be a certain amount of people who wish to brush up on their

Latin (I know many of these people myself and think they are great) but the vast majority of modern English speaking people simply do not.

The bigger elephant in the room here are all of the Catholics who now have been displaced by the new Mass translation. I like to think of them fondly as the old "We believe" crowd. What is their motivation to gather together now and say "I believe"? For it is quite reasonable and proper to say "I believe" all by myself.

Faith, Reason, and the New Mass Translation.

Faith, Reason, and the New Mass Translation.

Faith, Reason, and the New Mass Translation.

A $5 WORD CAN BE COSTLY

One of the innovations in the new Mass is something I should really like in my brain yet just plain old bothers me in my gut. It is the use of a fancy new "$5 word" in the Creed. As a theologian I like $5 dollar words. After all, isn't explaining $5 words what you really need a theologian around for in the first place? Yet as a layman, I was always taught that the Creed was something special. And that since the people who came before me had shed their blood for every word in it I should be willing to do the same. Of course those were the grand old days of the last century when testosterone was still welcome in the chapel. So people ran around saying militaristic things like that all the time. It got to be so bad that, out of fear of the testosterone, many parishes took the word "men" out of the Creed altogether. This caused me to wonder if a parrot happened to fly into one of these parishes and say "for us and for our salvation" if that bird would then be a parishioner too?

Sometimes though a $5 word can be costly. Take when it says in the new creed "consubstantial with the Father" where in the old version it said "one in being with the Father." "Consubstantial" after all is a pretty fancy word and the apologists for the new Mass say it will make things much more clear. Guess those guys really are theologians (because only a theologian could have a thought like that!). Does using fancy words that only a theologian can understand really make things more clear? It does if your goal is to attract more

Faith, Reason, and the New Mass Translation.

theologians to Mass. As a matter of fact I think the new Mass in general is a tremendous tool for attracting more theologians into the Church. However, I always thought before that we wanted to attract the average person who speaks modern English into the Church. Guess I was mistaken again.

The problem is that even for a theologian the word "consubstantial" can get a bit tricky sometimes. Let's say that you have a Lutheran friend who has studied some theology. You take him along to the new Mass one Sunday and he hears the new creed. Afterwards he remarks to you:

> "I always thought that the whole 'consubstantiation' thing was what separated Lutherans and Catholics.

Faith, Reason, and the New Mass Translation.

> Isn't it great that we are now making such ecumenical progress!"

Who can spot the problem here? You see in Trinitarian theology, which this passage in the creed is referring to, "consubstantial" is the right term to use. However, in Eucharistic theology consubstantiation is not Catholic belief. It is rather the Lutheran belief that the bread and wine are only the body and blood of Christ during the liturgy. In Eucharistic theology as Catholics we believe in transubstantiation and not consubstantiation. Seems a little bit complicated does it not? I even know some pretty good theology students who missed that one on the exam! Yet now for supposed "greater clarity" we all get to be the theology student!

Faith, Reason, and the New Mass Translation.

The fact is that asking people to use words they do not fully understand brings confusion rather than clarity. It makes them all like that parrot who just happened to fly into Mass and recite the creed. Modern people need to be engaged where they are at through the use of language they can understand. That was the brilliance of the "One in being." For it took a very complex theological idea and made it clear, simple, and understandable for the masses. It was a phrase you could understand. One that felt good in your gut when you said it. One that gave you something to believe in and to fight for.

Erudite words like "consubstantial" are fine for the theologians. However, the mission of the Church is not to get more theologians to come to Mass! It is to get the average modern person who is troubled by the world and looking for some meaning in his or her life to come to Mass! The new Mass in this way has made Christ less accessible and not more accessible. It has effectively shut some of those windows that the Second Vatican Council sought to open up.

It seems a $5 word can indeed be costly.

Faith, Reason, and the New Mass Translation.

Faith, Reason, and the New Mass Translation.

THE ALL AND THE MANY

Among the changes of the new Mass the "all" to "many" of the Eucharistic consecration prayer is perhaps the most theologically disturbing. And this is so for several reasons. The first is that the liturgy of the Eucharist is for a Catholic really at the heart and centre of the Mass. For the liturgy of the Word, because of varying scripture readings, changes each day but the liturgy of the Eucharist remains more constant.

This constant expression is also in reality the central expression of the Christian faith in that it answers the burning question of who Christ died for. The Novus Ordo mass of 1973 thus has the priest celebrant say:

Faith, Reason, and the New Mass Translation.

> "Take this, all of you, and drink from it: this is the cup of my blood, the blood of the new and everlasting covenant. It will be shed for you and for **all** so that sins may be forgiven. Do this in memory of me."

While the New mass translation has the priest celebrant say:

> "Take this, all of you, and drink from it: this is the cup of my blood, the blood of the new and everlasting covenant. It will be shed for you and for **many** so that sins may be forgiven. Do this in memory of me."

The reason I say "theologically disturbing" is that anyone who has studied Christian theology knows that Christ's sacrificial offering on the Cross was made for all. Indeed Second Corinthians chapter 5 verses 14-15 clearly states:

> "For the love of Christ impels us, once we have come to the conviction that **one died for all**; therefore, all have died. **Christ indeed died for all**, so that those who live might no longer live for themselves but for him who for their sake died and was raised."

This being the case, why change the prayer to "many" from "all"?

The stated reason of the Church is that it more accurately literally translates the Latin "pro multis" used in the consecration of the wine in the old Roman rite Latin mass. And the fact is that most scholars of such things agree that this is indeed the case.

Interestingly enough, the Church when questioned on whether it believes that Christ only died for many and not for all, known in theology as "Limited Atonement", is quick to point out that it does in fact hold that Christ died for all yet is then just as quick to insist that we now must use the term "many" in the consecration prayer!

This in reality cuts not just at the heart of Christian belief but at the very heart of the Church's whole argument for a literal translation from the Latin. For the literal translation of the Latin "pro multis" is in fact "many" yet the use of "many" to replace "all" clearly makes it seem to a modern English speaking person like the Church now believes in Limited Atonement!

This is not only a scandal to Catholics but a scandal to other Christians as well. For they know that the Bible clearly teaches that Christ died for all, yet they also know that the Catholics are now saying "many." This creates a dangerous confusion that might cause scandal and harm to Christianity as a whole. And why might this be the case? Because modern English speaking people tend to think and speak in modern English! (and not ancient Latin). Thus, if one wishes to communicate important theological truths to them it would be advisable to do the same.

If there is one moment in the new

Mass that makes me cringe and really say "this is not the faith of my youth" this is it. Yet in life it is often not where you arrive at but how you get there that is most important.

The Church of my youth was a place of religious and moral clarity. It was a place where you showed reverence toward the tabernacle or were immediately called on it. It was a place where you were given clear moral guidance and taught that your "yes" should mean "yes" and your "no" should mean "no" and that anything else was from the evil one (Matthew 5:37).

Therefore, even more disturbing than the new Mass translation itself is that in the aftermath of the new Mass translation I have seen churchmen stand up and tell me with a straight face that "many" really means "all" and that although we still mean "all" we must now say "many"? In the days of my youth such explanations were not those of the churchmen but of the lawyers and the politicians. Later, as I began to study philosophy, I realized that the lawyers and the politicians really belong to the same group known to the ancient Greeks as the Sophists.

Sophistry began as a good institution designed to equip the average man with the ability to speak in public so he might become a citizen capable of engaging in the democratic assemblies of the day. Yet the institution eventually deteriorated into something which still resembled its old self yet had become quite harmful.

The reason for this is that a good

Sophist was a man who would take a truth about how to have a better society for all and then connect it to some form of persuasive speech so it might be accepted and become a reality. While a bad Sophist would take a self-serving lie and connect it to some form of persuasive speech so that he might gain personal advantage at the cost of the public good from it. Thus the separation of "truth" from "persuasion" became decried as "Sophistry" even up until our own day (particularly with regard to those lawyers and politicians).

Here it is interesting to note that the Novus Ordo Mass came along in history right around the time of Watergate. Now if any of you can remember Watergate it was certainly not a distinguishing time for the politicians. In fact, the clear nature of

Faith, Reason, and the New Mass Translation.

the new modern English Mass translation of 1973 stood in a stark contrast to the sophistry and corruption of the Watergate scandal.

As a young boy who had just come into the age of reason around 1973 the message was clear. Politics were a place of lies and deceit yet the Church was a place of truth and clarity. Politicians used fancy words to tell lies while churchmen used simple words to tell the truth. "All" meant "all" and "many" meant "many" and the only person who might even try to convince you of something different would be wearing a fancy suit and certainly not a habit or a vestment!

However, here in the wake of the new Mass translations of 2011 I am not so sure about all of this anymore. For the place of clarity and truth that was the Church seems to me much more like the place of lies and deceit that is politics. And this for me is the saddest reality of all. For it is one thing to change the translation of the Mass, yet quite another thing to change the meaning and position of the Church in society as a whole!

Oh where is the Church of my youth? Where your yes meant "yes" and your no meant "no" and anything else was clearly and simply from the evil one.

Faith, Reason, and the New Mass Translation.

Faith, Reason, and the New Mass Translation.

A TALE OF TWO TRADITIONS

Last weekend I attended two rather interesting, and I think telling, events. One was a talk by a famous Jesuit priest at the Catholic parish where I grew up and the other was a fund raiser for a local Islamic high school. Although it was not obviously apparent at the time, both events hold much deeper connections than just happening to be a part of my weekend schedule.

These connections date back to the twelfth and thirteenth centuries in the figures of two outstanding scholars. The first is the great Islamic scholar Averroes. Born in Cordoba Spain in 1126 AD Averroes went on to become one of the greatest thinkers of his day.

Highly skilled in Law, Philosophy, Theology, Astronomy, Medicine, Mathematics, Music, and many other sciences Averroes was, in fact, one of the greatest thinkers of all time.

However, ironically, his greatest contributions have perhaps been to Christianity rather than to Islam. This is because Averroes was "The Commentator" on "The Philosopher" himself Aristotle. And these very terms "The Commentator" and "The Philosopher" were coined by none other than the great thirteenth century Catholic scholar Saint Thomas Aquinas. For much of what Aquinas learned about Aristotle in the thirteenth century was due to the commentaries Averroes wrote on him in the twelfth century.

Faith, Reason, and the New Mass Translation.

A common theme between these two great thinkers is the relationship between faith and reason. Averroes held that both philosophy and religion were ways to Truth. A radical idea in the Islam of his day. And although Christianity did have an existing tradition of faith and reason Aquinas was forced to defend it against many attacks. Ultimately perfecting the idea of the theological syllogism.

A syllogism is a form of argumentation invented by Aristotle. It is composed of several statements, known as premises, which are related to one another logically.

Major Premise: All men are mortal
Minor Premise: Socrates is a man
Conclusion: Socrates is mortal.

In a normal syllogism the premises can

be proven through observation and reason (as indeed is the case here). However, in a theological syllogism this is sometimes not the case. What Aquinas pointed out, in the famous controversy on the topic at the University of Paris, is that although the premises of a theological syllogism sometimes can't be proven by observation and reason they can find their proofs in Sacred Scripture and Tradition. Therefore, the new logic of Aristotle can be applied to theology in the form of a theological syllogism!

Thus, a balance in the roles of philosophy and theology was struck in Christianity. And it is a balance which has remained with us until our own day. This is attested to in the encyclical of Pope John Paul II from 1998 entitled "Fides et Ratio" (Faith and Reason). For in it he states:

Faith, Reason, and the New Mass Translation.

> "Faith and reason are like two wings on which the human spirit rises to the contemplation of truth; and God has placed in the human heart a desire to know the truth—in a word, to know himself—so that, by knowing and loving God, men and women may also come to the fullness of truth about themselves."

The beautiful imagery of a bird rising to the contemplation of the Truth used by Pope John Paul II here is a clear message that it is only through a balance of faith and reason that a religion can thrive. For what can a bird with only one wing do besides spiral toward its own demise?

Why is reason so important to faith? Quite simply because faith alone, unbalanced by any other force or factor, can become turned in on itself and quite dangerous to both those inside and outside of it. This I have seen many times in my own life in various versions of both Christianity and Islam. Be it Jonestown or 9/11 we have had several recent examples of faith unchecked by reason becoming destructive.

Thus, the struggle to ascend to truth remains for us all. And the brilliance of Averroes High School and the movement behind it is that they have tapped into one of the great figures in the history of this struggle. An Islamic figure who is also one of the pillars of European society because of his insistence that faith should be guided by reason!

Faith, Reason, and the New Mass Translation.

At my Catholic gathering this past weekend unfortunate comments were made. "Professors" were derided for teaching relativism and attacking faith. As a professor of Philosophy myself I found such comments curious because in just about every philosophy textbook I have seen it is indeed the refutation of relativism that is one of the first orders of business. And in my own courses it is indeed the first order of business (before we even open the textbook).

In contrast, at the Averroes High School event speakers were lauded for their academic credentials and indeed a non-Islamic professor was the keynote speaker. And after all was said and done I had to admit that as an educator I felt somewhat derided at a Catholic event and rather appreciated at a, primarily, Islamic event.

Faith, Reason, and the New Mass Translation.

And this is not the first time I have encountered a rather anti-academic environment in Christian circles of late. Add to this the recent new English translation of the Catholic Mass from a clear modern English to an archaic English with Latin grammar and one cannot help but see a trend developing.

It is indeed ironic that just as the Catholic faith seems to be forgetting its great tradition of reason some brave visionaries in the Islamic faith are working to rediscover their own. And this is even more ironic in light of the fact that in many ways Averroes was the seed of thought for Aquinas in his great defense of the theological syllogism.

It was indeed then an interesting weekend. A weekend in which I

Faith, Reason, and the New Mass Translation.

found out that my own tradition has something to learn from another. A weekend in which I came to know about a new movement to combine faith and reason. A weekend in which I encountered many hospitable and good people at both events for whom I am all grateful.

Although Averroes High School certainly seems to be a primarily Islamic institution at the moment there is certainly a hope, because of their respect for both faith and reason, that it might one day become an American institution. And perhaps just another example of how immigrants from other lands often serve as the leaven that causes America to once again rise.

Faith, Reason, and the New Mass Translation.

Faith, Reason, and the New Mass Translation.

Comments I made on "Lifesite News" with regard to Faith Reason, and the Church's teaching authority.

(http://www.lifesitenews.com/blog/popes-guidance-to-bishops-on-abortion-has-serious-implications-for-irelands).

Faith, Reason, and the New Mass Translation.

TEACHING AUTHORITY

Notice that by giving this guideline the Church is not bullying politicians into being pro-life by threatening to withhold the Eucharist from them, a charge I am sure some will make, but rather engaging in an act of mercy by seeking to protect people who encourage and aid in abortion from being cursed through an unworthy reception of the Eucharist. And yes I did say "cursed" because Sacred Scripture indicates this:

> "Therefore anyone who eats the bread or drinks the cup of the lord unworthily...is eating and drinking his own condemnation"
> (1 Corinthians 11:27-29).

Faith, Reason, and the New Mass Translation.

Notice the call to not only follow the Church out of faith but for right reasoning (and the suggestion that the two are really the same thing): "The Magisterium and right reasoning is needed!" Here we have a truth which Blessed John Paul II made very clear to us in his letter "Fides et Ratio" (Faith and Reason).

While the Church is good about giving moral guidance it is often not so good at encouraging the use of reason. Particularly when it fails to engage its own people over important matters and instead appeals to the obedience of faith to bring about adherence. The recent imposition of a new English translation of the Mass being a prime example of this. Here we see how the failure of the Church to move in accordance with its own values opens up its teaching as a whole to doubt.

Faith, Reason, and the New Mass Translation.

The message being that one cannot have it both ways. One either values reason over blind faith or one does not. And if the Magisterium wishes us to use right reason then it should model this behavior to us by engaging in the use of reason itself (rather than calling for blind faith).

Pope John Paul II did this with regard to the Life issues in *Evangelium Vitae*. He did this because he knew that each time the Church fails to move in accord with reason it chips away at its own teaching authority (the very teaching authority he worked so hard to strengthen). Here I am calling the Church to a life of integrity. The integrity of faith and reason it must have in order to fulfill its mission.

The debacle of the new Mass

translation, or more specifically how its implementation was handled, has wide reaching effects. The Creed has been changed, trust has been broken, and blind faith has triumphed over reasoned discourse.

If the Church thinks it has moved beyond these matters it is sadly mistaken. For the Church has in fact alienated many of the people it needs most in today's troubled world. People who believe that every word in the Creed is worth fighting for, people who can think critically, people who know that "Faith and reason are two wings on which the human spirit rises to the contemplation of truth." And that a bird with only one wing cannot ascend toward Truth but only spiral towards its own demise.

Faith, Reason, and the New Mass Translation.

Faith, Reason, and the New Mass Translation.

CONCLUSION

There are several issues which arise when investigating the new Mass translation. I would break them down into the four categories of product, process, implementation, and message.

Those questions of product ask things like, "How good is the translation?" And, "How will it help the Church move forward in the modern world?" These lead to questions about whether a literal or a literary translation is better. Yet all these question really beg the question of "What is the purpose of the new Mass translation?" Or "Who is the Church hoping to speak to with it?"

If the hope of the Church is the evangelization of the modern world then it is sadly mistaken in putting forth such an archaic literal translation for this purpose. In fact, the Church would have been much better off in simply keeping with the wonderful modern literary translation of the 1973 Novus Ordo Mass.

This leads to the question of the process of the creation of the new Mass translation. Clearly the legitimate process on the local level was frustrated in this case by an intervention, some might even say a "hijacking", by the Vatican Congregation for Divine Worship. And clearly this intervention violated the Church's own standard for social justice—Subsidiarity.

We then move on to the implementation of the new Mass translation. A time in which the

Faith, Reason, and the New Mass Translation.

classic story of "The Emperor's New Clothes" often came to mind. A time when we were told that even though "many" really means "all" we must now, for the sake of clarity, say "many."

We then have the issue of the message that the new Mass translation sends to the modern world. A message which seems to be that to be a Catholic means to go to Mass on Sundays and say some rather unreasonable things. Whether it be giving a strange response to a greeting by the priest, using big words you do not really understand in the creed, or making insensitive comments about needing a "roof" in order to receive Christ in the Eucharist. With all of these things clearly being a hindrance, and certainly not a help, for the average modern person wishing to explore the Catholic faith.

Oh where is the Church of faith and reason that our beloved Saint John Paul II once envisioned? And how can the new evangelization he called for now move forward when even many life-long Catholics, like myself, can barely stand to attend Mass? It is indeed the issue of the effect that the new English Mass translation is having on existing Catholics that is closest to my own heart. For if one accepts the premise of "Lex Orandi, Lex Credendi" then certain things must logically follow.

Those of us brought up in the post Vatican II Church were brought up in the prayer of the 1973 Novus Ordo Mass. And what follows from the prayer of the 1973 Novus Ordo Mass is the belief of the 1973 Novus Ordo

Faith, Reason, and the New Mass Translation.

Mass (for as we pray so we believe). I was born in 1964 so when I was asked at the Sacrament of Confirmation to make an adult consent to the Catholic faith the consent I made was to the belief which followed from the 1973 Novus Ordo Mass.

I fought for this belief often in harsh circumstances. I gave up, or was denied, personal and professional opportunities. I served the Church by teaching this belief in CCD classes, youth groups, and at my university campus ministry. I wrote many letters to the editor of the newspaper defending this belief. And, if it had become necessary, I would even have had been willing to have had my own blood shed in order to defend each and every word in the Creed!

However, at Advent 2011 the belief

of the Church I fought for all those years was suddenly changed. And not by a repressive government or communist revolution, but by a Vatican Congregation! A Congregation which by its very actions violated one of the Church's most important principles of Social Justice—Subsidiarity!

And Catholic lay people like myself are hardly alone in our assessment of the new English Mass translation. For in a recent survey of Catholic priests 59% of them said they did not like the new translation and more than 1/3 of them said they "strongly disagree" that the new translation is an improvement over its predecessor. Further, a full 80% of the Catholic priests surveyed said they agreed with an assessment of the new Mass translation as being "awkward and distracting" and 61% of them said the new Mass translation needs to be revised "urgently." [viii]

Yet even more disturbing than the numbers is the article's assertion about the damage to the relationship between Catholic priests and the Vatican that the new English Mass translation has caused. For because the new Mass translation was conceived and implemented without legitimate local input, as the principle of Subsidiarity calls for, many priests now feel that the Vatican has not kept faith with them. They, further, feel like they are now being forced to choose between loyalty to the Vatican and feeding the spiritual needs of their parishioners. So clearly the Church has engaged in a damaging process here even in terms of its relationship to its own clerics!

Faith, Reason, and the New Mass Translation.

There are a great deal of burning questions brought about by an examination of the new English Mass translation. With perhaps the most burning one of all being "How can the current hurt and division in the Church now be made right?" Sadly, because of the poor process engaged in by the Church here, both in terms of the creation and implementation of the new Mass translation, a great deal of damage has been done. Trust built up over decades, and even lifetimes, has been broken and people faithful to the Church of their youth have been lost. So we must first, unfortunately, acknowledge that things can never really be the same again. That the damage that has been done is indeed quite deep and abiding.

However, certain steps could be made to at least begin the healing process. First, the Vatican could acknowledge that this whole situation has been handled poorly and that Catholics in the English speaking world deserve to be able to worship God in the manner to which they have become accustomed. Second, the 1973 Novus Ordo Mass could be restored for those who wish to practice it. And, based upon current surveys of both clerics and lay people, this is, in fact, a great majority of those in the Church today (not to even mention the many who have left the Church yet wish to return). Third, an investigation could go on into who hijacked the legitimate process for a second English translation? The 2001 order to change the rules of the game in the English translation went on during the reign of Pope John Paul II yet at this time he was ailing greatly in his sufferings for the Church and must have had to rely greatly on others. Who were these others and what motives did they hold?

The Church's mission is to make Christ present in the modern world. Both the new Mass translation itself and the poor process of its creation and implementation have now become a hindrance in this. With the current spiritual thirst in the world for meaning and purpose we are in a great position today to have many people take a second look at the Catholic faith. Thus, now more than ever, we need a modern and accessible English translation of the Mass. The Novus Ordo Mass of 1973 is such a translation.

Let us today honor Saint John Paul II through a renewal of his vision of a Church of faith and reason going forth

Faith, Reason, and the New Mass Translation.

to evangelize the modern world. And may Saint John Paul II, the Pope of Faith and Reason, pray for us all!

Faith, Reason, and the New Mass Translation.

Faith, Reason, and the New Mass Translation.

[i] Gaspari, Antonio "Ten Years After The Scihsm" as found in Inside The Vatican Magazine August-September, 1998, p.20.

[ii] Carusa, Alberto "Rome's New "Game Plan": Heal The Lefebvre Schism" as found in Inside The Vatican Magazine May, 2000, p.17.

[iii] The Declaration Instauratio Liturgica, of January 25, 1974, by the Sacred Congregation for the Doctrine of the Faith, clarified the confusion over "pro multis" in the following way.

> *"The liturgical reform which has been carried out in accordance with the Constitution of the Second Vatican Council has made certain changes in the essential formulae of the sacramental rites. These new expressions, like the other ones, have had to be translated into modern languages in such a way that the original sense finds expression in the idiom proper to each language."*

[iv] Letter Of His Holiness Benedict Xvi To The Bishops On The Occasion Of The Publication Of The Apostolic Letter "Motu

Faith, Reason, and the New Mass Translation.

Proprio Data" Summorum Pontificum:On The Use of the Roman Liturgy Prior to the Reform of 1970.

[v] From an Associated Press article found in Haaretz online magazine January 24, 2009.
http://www.haaretz.com/jewish-world/2.209/pope-lifts-excommunication-of-bishop-who-denied-holocaust-1.268759

[vi] Congregation For Divine Worship And The Discipline Of The Sacraments Fifth Instruction "For The Right Implementation Of The Constitution On The Sacred Liturgy Of The Second Vatican Council" (Sacrosanctum Concilium, Art. 36) Liturgiam Authenticam On The Use Of Vernacular Languages In The Publication Of The Books Of The Roman Liturgy.

[vii] CCC 1883.

[viii] McElwee, Joshua "Priests dislike new Mass translations, survey says" as found in National Catholic Reporter May 21, 2013 online edition.

ABOUT THE AUTHOR

John C. Wilhelmsson is an author, publisher, professor of philosophy at San Jose State University, and successful businessman. As both a working philosopher and Catholic speaker he is known for his enthusiastic style and thoughtful and independent interpretations. A life-long resident of the Santa Clara Valley, which he still likes to think of as the "Valley of the Heart's Delight," John currently lives just close enough to the university to walk there on the mornings he teaches.

Faith, Reason, and the New Mass Translation.

Faith, Reason, and the New Mass Translation.

BASIC ORDINARY TEXT OF THE 1973 EDITION OF THE NOVUS ORDO MASS

GREETING

Priest: "The Lord be with you."

People: "And also with you."

Faith, Reason, and the New Mass Translation.

PENITENTIAL ACT

Form A

"I confess to almighty God,

and to you, my brothers and sisters,

that I have sinned

through my own fault,

in my thoughts and in my words,

in what I have done,

and in what I have failed to do;

and I ask blessed Mary, ever virgin,

all the angels and saints,

and you, my brothers and sisters,

to pray for me to the Lord, our God."

Form B

Priest:

"Lord, we have sinned against you: Lord, have mercy."

People:

"Lord, have mercy."

Priest:

"Lord, show us your mercy and love."

People:

"And grant us your salvation."

Faith, Reason, and the New Mass Translation.

GLORIA

"Glory to God in the highest,
and peace to his people on earth.
Lord God, heavenly King,
almighty God and Father,
we worship you, we give you thanks,
we praise you for your glory.
Lord Jesus Christ,
only Son of the Father,
Lord God, Lamb of God,
you take away the sin of the world:
have mercy on us;
you are seated at the right hand of the
Father: receive our prayer.
For you alone are the Holy One,
you alone are the Lord,
you alone are the Most High, Jesus
Christ, with the Holy Spirit,
in the glory of God the Father.
Amen."

Faith, Reason, and the New Mass Translation.

Faith, Reason, and the New Mass Translation.

NICENE CREED

"We believe in one God,
the Father, the Almighty,
maker of heaven and earth,
of all that is seen and unseen.
We believe in one Lord, Jesus Christ,
the only Son of God,
eternally begotten of the Father,
God from God, Light from Light,
true God from true God,
begotten, not made,
one in Being with the Father.
Through him all things were made.
For us men and for our salvation
he came down from heaven:
by the power of the Holy Spirit
he was born of the Virgin Mary,
and became man.
For our sake
he was crucified under Pontius Pilate;
he suffered, died, and was buried.

Faith, Reason, and the New Mass Translation.

On the third day he rose again
in fulfillment of the Scriptures;
he ascended into heaven and is seated
at the right hand of the Father.
He will come again in glory
to judge the living and the dead,
and his kingdom will have no end.
We believe in the Holy Spirit,
the Lord, the giver of life,
who proceeds
from the Father and the Son.
With the Father and the Son
he is worshipped and glorified.
He has spoken through the Prophets.
We believe in one holy catholic
and apostolic Church.
We acknowledge one baptism
for the forgiveness of sins.
We look for the resurrection
of the dead,
and the life of the world to come.
Amen."

SUSCIPIAT DOMINUS

"May the Lord accept the sacrifice

at your hands

for the praise and glory of his name,

for our good,

and the good of all his Church."

Faith, Reason, and the New Mass Translation.

Faith, Reason, and the New Mass Translation.

PREFACE DIALOGUE

Priest: "The Lord be with you."

People: "And also with you."

Priest: "Lift up your hearts."

People: "We lift them up to the Lord."

Priest: "Let us give thanks to the Lord our God."

People: "It is right to give him thanks and praise."

SANCTUS

"Holy, holy, holy Lord,

God of power and might.

Heaven and earth are

full of your glory.

Hosanna in the highest.

Blessed is he who comes

in the name of the Lord.

Hosanna in the highest."

Faith, Reason, and the New Mass Translation.

MYSTERY OF FAITH

Priest:

"Let us proclaim the mystery of faith."

People:

A – "Christ has died, Christ is risen, Christ will come again."

B – "Dying you destroyed our death, rising you restored our life. Lord Jesus, come in glory."

C – "When we eat this bread

and drink this cup,

we proclaim your death,

Lord Jesus,

until you come in glory."

D – "Lord, by your cross

and resurrection,

you have set us free.

You are the Savior of the World."

Faith, Reason, and the New Mass Translation.

SIGN OF PEACE

Priest:

"The peace of the Lord be with you always."

People:

"And also with you."

Faith, Reason, and the New Mass Translation.

Faith, Reason, and the New Mass Translation.

ECCE AGNUS DEI

Priest:

"This is the Lamb of God

who takes away

the sins of the world.

Happy are those who are called

to his supper."

All:

"Lord, I am not worthy

to receive you,

but only say the word

and I shall be healed."

Faith, Reason, and the New Mass Translation.

Faith, Reason, and the New Mass Translation.

CONCLUDING RITE

Priest:

"The Lord be with you."

People:

"And also with you."

www.ingramcontent.com/pod-product-compliance
Lightning Source LLC
Chambersburg PA
CBHW071705040426
42446CB00011B/1924